SUNDAY SPORT

NAUGHTY CARTOONS

Also from Sphere Books:
THE BEST OF THE SUNDAY SPORT

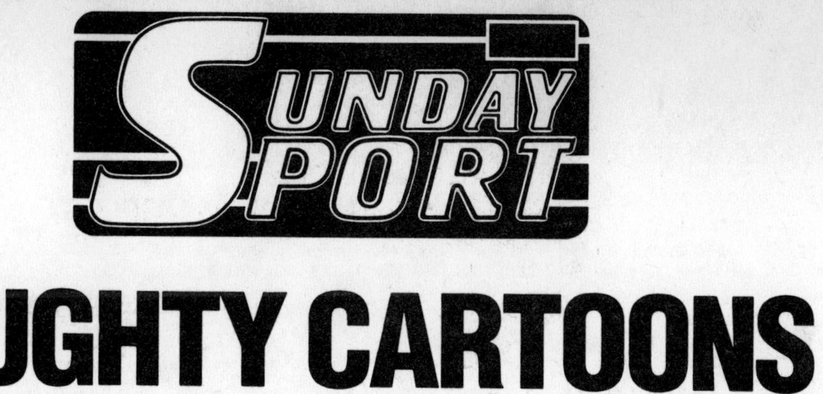

NAUGHTY CARTOONS

Sphere Books Limited

A Sphere Book

First published in Great Britain in 1990
by Sphere Books Limited, a division of
Macdonald & Co (Publishers) Ltd
London & Sydney

Printed in Great Britain by
The Guernsey Press Co. Ltd., Guernsey, Channel Islands.

ISBN 0 7474 0698 7

Sphere Books Ltd
A division of Macdonald & Co (Publishers) Ltd
Orbit House
1 New Fetter Lane
London EC4A 1AR

A member of Maxwell Macmillan Pergamon Publishing Corporation

"IS THAT ALL YOU EVER THINK ABOUT?"

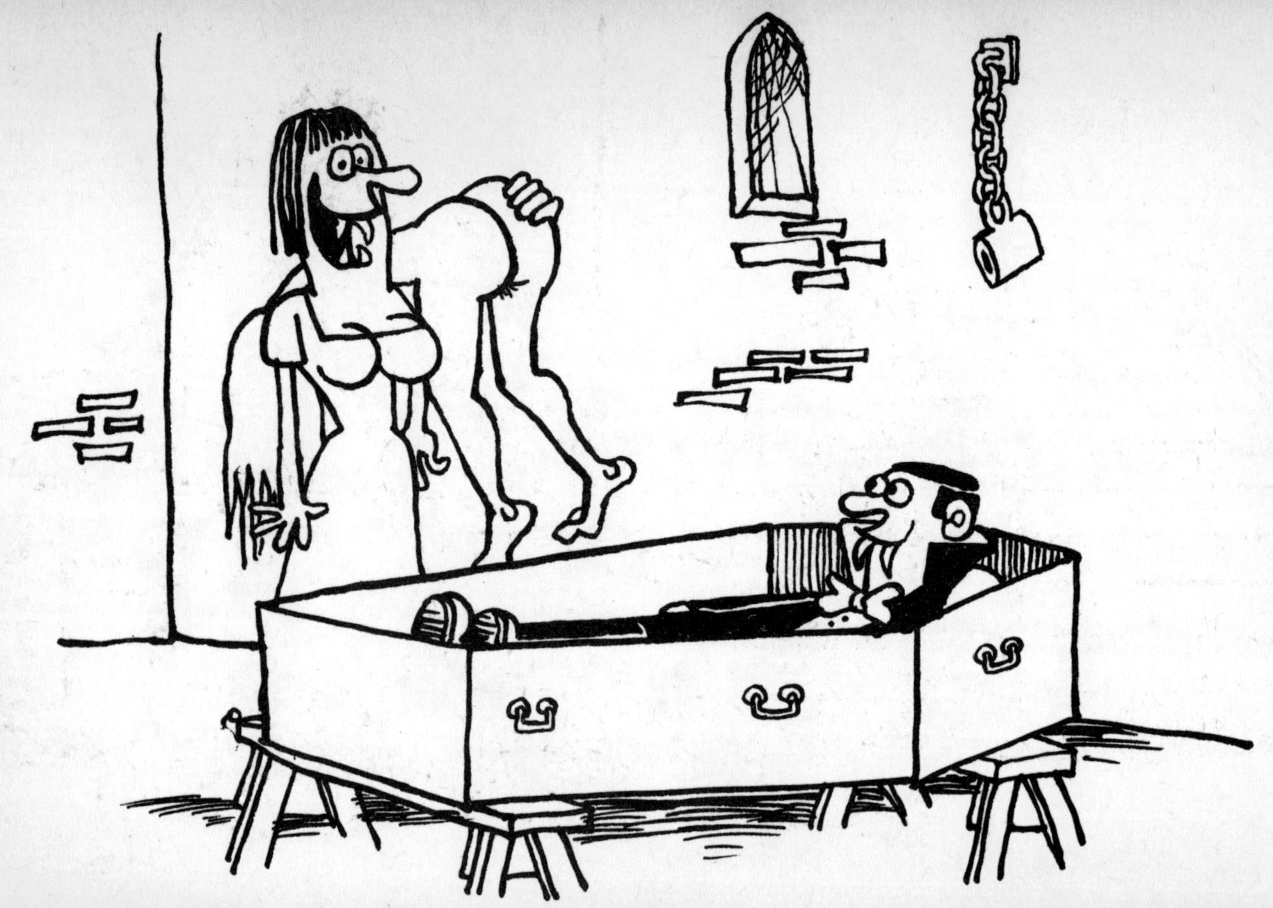

"BREAKFAST IN BED, DEAR?"

"SOMETIMES I WISH I'D NEVER MARRIED A BLEEDIN' WEREWOLF!"

WHAT DID YOU THINK TO IT, VIC?
IT WASN'T TOO BAD....
..ER... HOW CAN I PUT IT?
EXCHANGE YOUR VIDEOS
YOURS + £3
EROTICA 3
HIRE-A-VIDEO

.... ER.... IT'S LIKE MAKING LOVE TO THE SAME WOMAN!
XCHANGE YOUR VIDEOS
OURS + £3
EROTI 3
HIRE-A-VIDEO

... IT GOT BORING AFTER THE 500th TIME !!!!
HANGE YOUR IDEOS
+ £3
HIRE-A-VIDEO
FROM £1·50

"MY LAST EMPLOYER DIDN'T LIVE LONG ENOUGH TO GIVE ME A REFERENCE, BUT I'LL TELL YOU ONE THING - HE DIED HAPPY."

"And don't go mucking about with girls!"

INFLATABLE VOYEUR
(NON RAINCOAT MODEL)
DIS

"MAYBE YOU OVERDID IT. JUST PULL UP YOUR SKIRT AND SHOW A BIT OF LEG NEXT TIME."

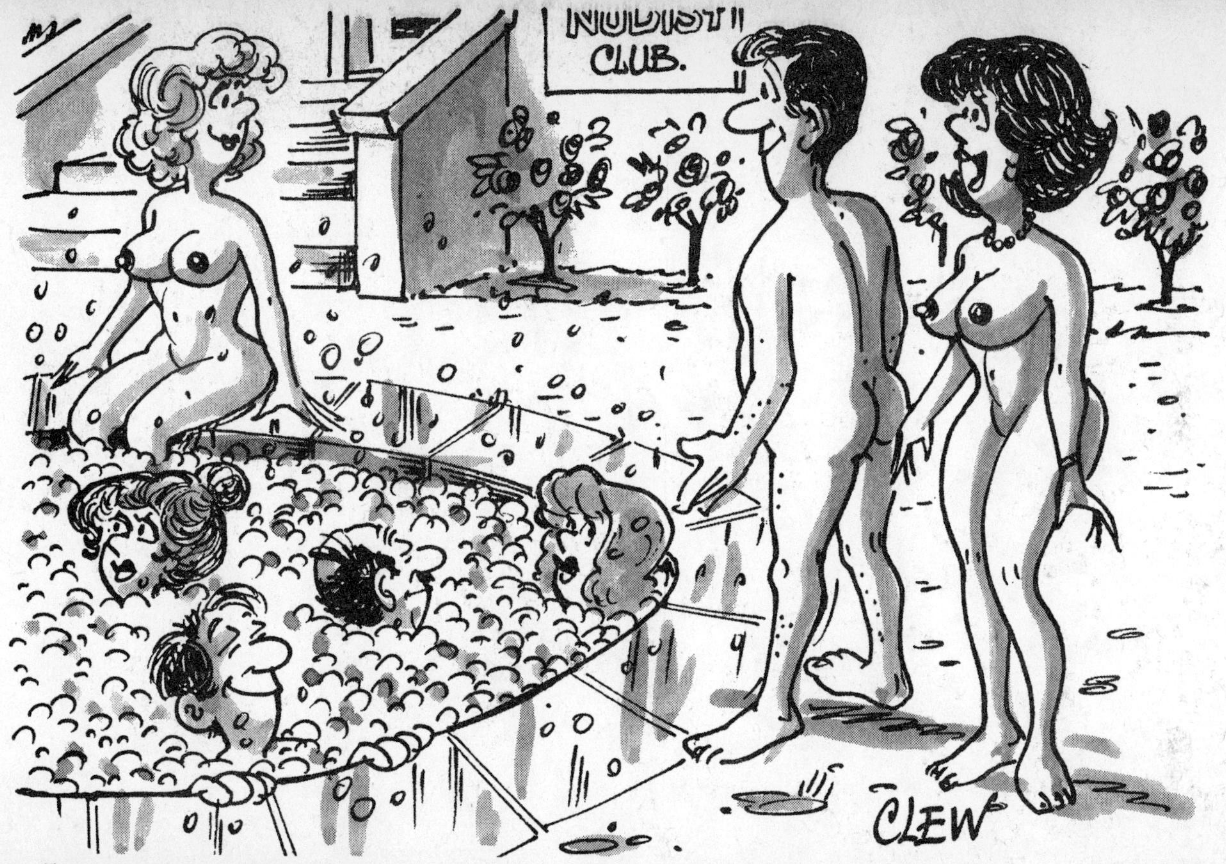

"NO, THIS ISN'T A JACUZZI – IT'S AN ORDINARY POOL .... BUT WE ALL HAD BAKED BEANS ON TOAST FOR LUNCH TODAY."

SPERM BANK
WARDS

"DON'T MOVE BOND! YOUR TEA-LADY DISGUISE IS BRILLIANT, BUT YOU FORGOT ONE THING!"

"IT'S NOT WHAT YOU THINK, OLD CHAP. I ALWAYS CARRY AN INFLATABLE RUBBER DOLL IN CASE OF EMERGENCIES."

'I'VE DECIDED TO GIVE YOU A SCREEN TEST, MISS BELLAMY. IF YOU'LL JUST GO BEHIND THAT SCREEN ....'

"YOU HAVEN'T MET MY WIFE, HAVE YOU? SHE'S A GREAT BELIEVER IN SPONTANEOUS SEX."

"REVEALING YOU'RE A TRANSVESTITE'S ALL VERY WELL, SERGEANT BULSTRODE, BUT YOU'VE CHOSEN A BLOODY ODD TIME TO DO IT!"

"MY WIFE DOESN'T UNDERSTAND ME."

"I FIND THAT A BLOW-UP DOLL IS MORE COMFORTABLE TO LIE ON THAN A SURF-BOARD."

"WITHOUT WISHING TO APPEAR UNCHARITABLE, I SOMETIMES WONDER IF MR JENNINGS EYESIGHT IS AS BAD AS HE CLAIMS"

"HOW SHOULD I KNOW WHO THE FATHER IS? YOU NEVER LET ME GO STEADY WITH ANYONE !"

"IT'S A MISS BRADY WHO WAS HERE ABOUT SIX MONTHS AGO. YOU APPARENTLY FILLED THE WRONG CAVITY."

BEST
BEFORE
1968
CLEW

"WHAT'S WRONG, MISS – NEVER SEEN A WINDOW CLEANER BEFORE?"

"I'VE JUST INVENTED A FAMILY PLANNING DEVICE."

"DO YOU MIND NOT WATCHING ME GET DRESSED!"

GET ME KNICKERS ORF ? HONESTLY, UGG - YOU CAN SOMETIMES
BE SO CRUDE."

"HEY, WILF THIS BLOKE SAYS YOU'RE SPELLIN' IT WRONG!"

"AND BECAUSE HE'S GOT A DICKEY HEART, I HAVE TO BLOW THE BLOODY THING UP FOR HIM!"

"KEEP PUMPING IT IN NIGEL! I CAN FEEL IT SWELLING AND GETTING HARDER WITH EVERY STROKE.... OOH, LOVELY!"

"OOPS ... SORRY, DOCTOR. I THOUGHT YOU'D HAVE FINISHED EXAMINING MY WIFE BY NOW"

'ADMITTEDLY IT WOULD BE HEARTLESS TO LET A POOR, HOMELESS ORPHAN WALK THE STREETS ON A NIGHT LIKE THIS – BUT COULDN'T YOU HAVE JUST LENT HER YOUR UMBRELLA ?"

'HE VIDIOED THE WEDDING CEREMONY AND RECEPTION FOR US ... AND FOR ONLY TWENTY QUID EXTRA HE'S VOLUNTEERED TO . . . . .'

5
7
CLEW

"COULD WE TRY SOMETHING APART FROM THE MISSIONARY POSITION TONIGHT??"

"THIS ISN'T WHAT I HAD IN MIND WHEN YOU SAID WE WERE GOING AWAY FOR A DIRTY WEEKEND!!"

"COR. STREWTH! I USED TO THINK THAT GETTING SAND BETWEEN YOUR TOES WAS UNCOMFORTABLE... !"

Video Vic by ZAKz

"I'M HAVING A WIFE-SWAPPING PARTY UP AT MY PLACE TONIGHT - AND YOU'RE BOTH INVITED."

"I SEE THAT 'AITCHES' AREN'T THE ONLY THINGS YOU DROP, MISS PERKINS."

"I TAKE IT THERE'S NOTHING ON T.V. THAT YOU WANT TO WATCH TONIGHT, DARLING."

"SO THAT'S WHY HE'S CALLED A PEER"

" BLOODY HELL, MISS - NO ANGEL IS PERFECT ! "

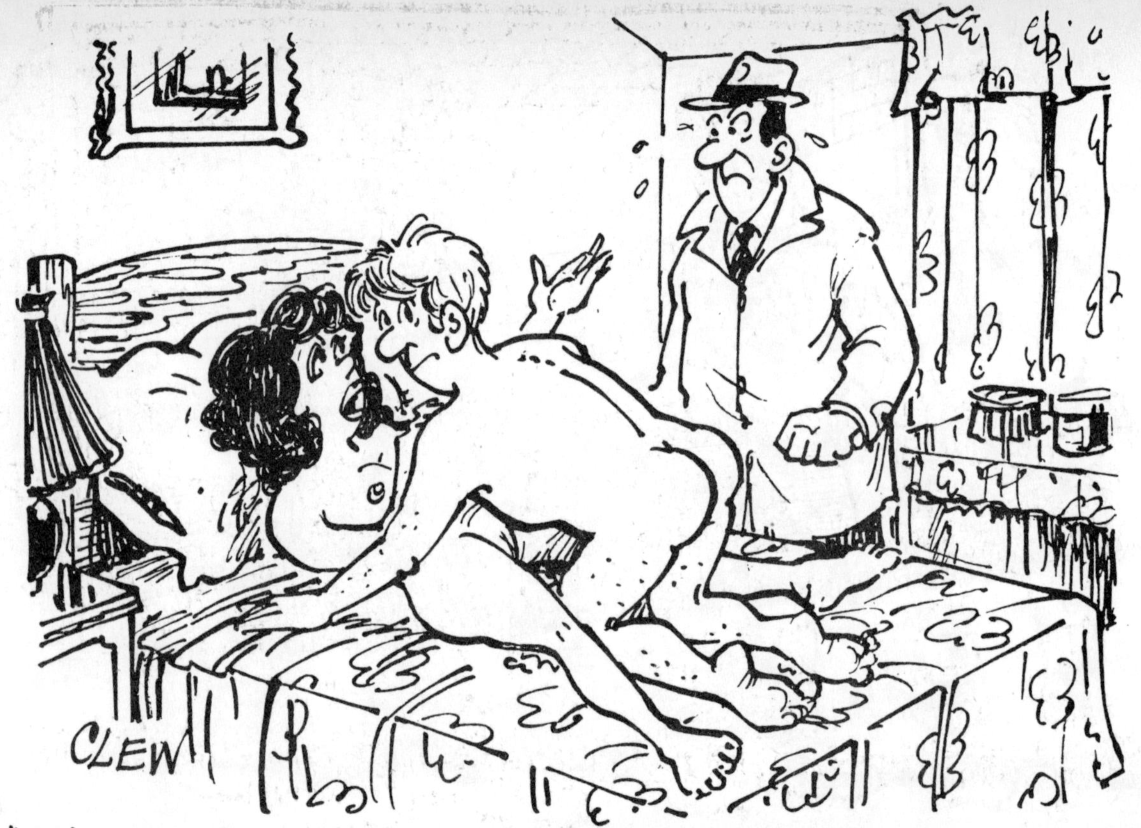

"I'VE GIVEN UP SMOKING! I'VE CUT DOWN ON DRINKING! I'M ON A STRICT DIET! FOR GOD'S SAKE, GEORGE– HOW MANY MORE SACRIFICES DO YOU WANT ME TO MAKE?"

"I THINK IT'S TIME YOU CAME OFF THOSE HORMONE TABLETS, TED"

"NOT ONLY IS MY WIFE A ROTTEN COOK, A ROTTEN HOUSEKEEPER AND A ROTTEN LAY – SHE'S ALSO A ROTTEN SHOT!"

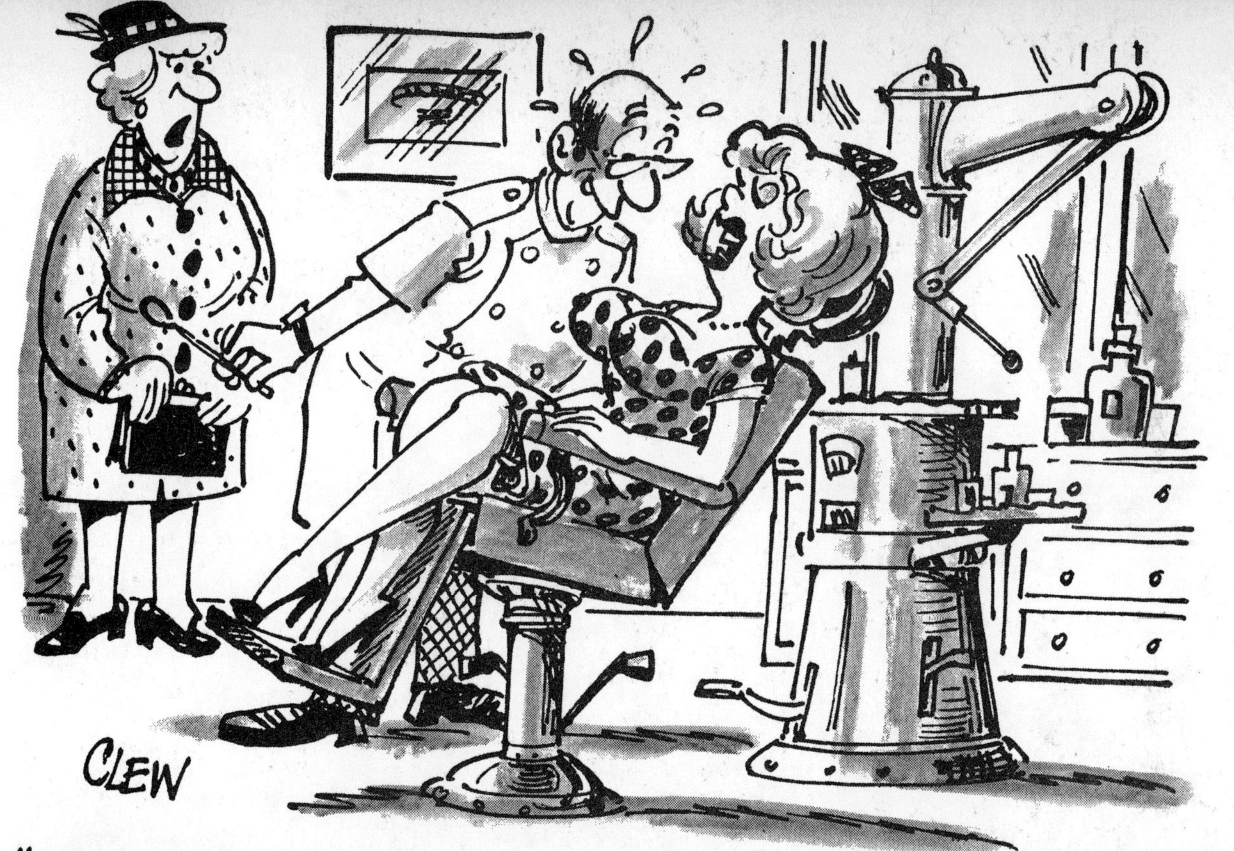

"WHEN YOU'VE GOT OVER YOUR SURPRISE AT THE WAY MY LITTLE GIRL HAS GROWN UP, I'D LIKE YOU TO EXAMINE HER TEETH"

"OOH, YOU RANDY DEVIL. I SUPPOSE YOU WANT TO DRAG ME OFF TO YOUR CAVE AND RAVISH ME"

CLEW

"YOU MUST BE JOKING, JILL. I'M TOO SHAGGED OUT FROM CLIMBING THIS BLOODY HILL!"

"HE MAY NOT BE INCREDIBLY GOOD LOOKING BUT HE'S GREAT AT ORAL SEX...."

"THIS IS SO EMBARRASSING – HOW COULD YOU LOSE THE KEY TO THE CHASTITY BELT?"

"AND JUST WHAT ARE YOU DOING UNDER YOUR DESK, ROBINSON ?"

"POOR GIRL'S DISAPPOINTED. SHE EXPECTED TO FIND THE WORLD'S BIGGEST HAMPTON AND A TWO-TON PAIR OF BOLLOCKS!"

"HOW MUCH A NIGHT IS THE BRIDAL SUITE?"

"DROP 'EM, GIRL! I SAID 'DROP 'EM'!"

"PUT AWAY THAT DISGUSTING BOOK, SIDNEY. WHAT ON EARTH CAN THE GENTLEMAN OPPOSITE BE THINKING?"

"SHE WANTS TO TRY THE COIL METHOD OF BIRTH CONTROL AND THINKS THIS ONE WILL BE BIG ENOUGH!"

"I SAW IT IN THE PAPER - IT'S AN ALL-GIRL EXPEDITION!"

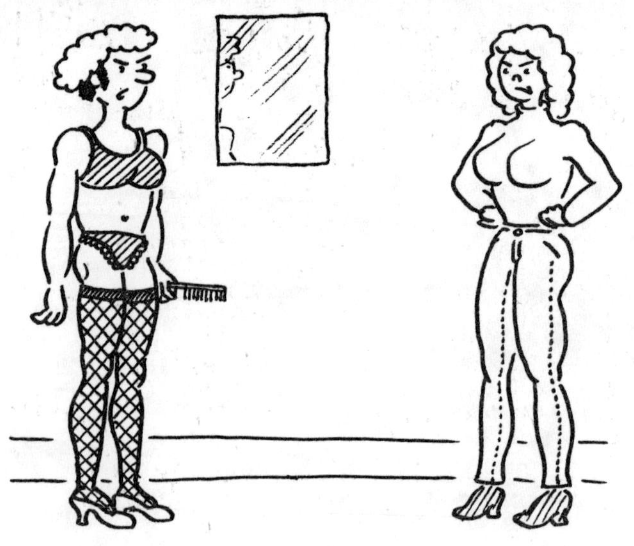

"WHAT'S THE MATTER? I DON'T COMPLAIN WHEN YOU WEAR TROUSERS, DO I

"YES, THEY DO SEEM TO FOLLOW YOU AROUND THE ROOM, DON'T THEY?"

"TROUBLE SIR — THEY'VE FORMED A UNION."

JUST
HARRIED
Paulus.

"SORRY, MISS - DID I SPLASH YOU ?"

"HEY, BUSTER – I THOUGHT YOU SAID YOU FANCIED A QUICK DIP!"

WHEN THE TAPE JAMS, WE CAN DO ONE OF THREE THINGS.

ONE, KICK IT AND RISK DAMAGING A £500 VIDEO MACHINE!

TWO, SEND FOR A VIDEO REPAIRMAN AND RISK A BIG BILL!
YELLOW PAGES

OR THREE, JUST SWITC
EVERYTHING OFF AND RIS
IT WITH ME!

CLEW

"NEW MEMBER."

"BUT I ALWAYS CHOOSE YOUR CLOTHES FOR YOU DEAR."

"IT USED TO BE HARDING'S NEWSAGENT'S.... THEN THEY STARTED SELLING RAUNCHY MAGAZINES...."

"DON'T WORRY IT WASN'T MY SOUL I SOLD HIM!"

WOW! LOOK AT THE SIZE OF THAT! .... LOOK AT THAT PAIR!

WHAT A FIRM PAIR! GO ON, MATE, HAVE A GOOD GROPE!!!

VIC! WHY CAN'T YOU READ A BOOK IN BED LIKE ANY NORMAL HUSBAND?

"THAT WAS VERY NAUGHTY OF YOU, SITTING BULL!"

"I PAID YOU £30, AND THE BLOODY THING LEAKS! DON'T GIVE ME THAT BULLSHIT ABOUT IT BEING A REALISTIC BUILT-IN FART!"

"THEY SENT THE WRONG ONE. IT SAYS 'EXTRA POWERFUL. FOR NYMPHOS ONLY'"

"THAT WAS ABSOLUTELY FANTASTIC, DARLING ! HOW WAS IT FOR YOU ?"

CLEW

"REMEMBER THE OLD DAYS WHEN WE USED TO BE A MÉNAGE À TROIS?

LOVERS' LANE
DIS

"HEY, PEDRO - WHAT'S ALL THAT MOANING AND GROANING I CAN HEAR?"

T'S PART OF A CANCELLED EXPORT ORDER FOR AN OLD-FASHIONED MIDDLE EASTERN GENT."

"STEPHANIE! MR RENTON! YOU'RE MISSING ALL THE FUN. WE'RE JUST ABOUT TO PLAY CHARADES."

"SEE? YOU'RE GRADUALLY OVERCOMING YOUR SHYNESS — NOW TRY IT WITH YOUR REAL HANDS."

"WE AGREED TO DOWN TOOLS TODAY, SCAB!"

"ME, FANCY HER? WHATEVER GAVE YOU THAT IDEA?

"I WANT TO REPORT A PEEPING TOM!"

"DARLING, I'VE GOT A LITTLE CONFESSION...."

"DO YOU HAVE TO EAT YOUR STICK OF ROCK LIKE THAT?"

"SORRY FIDEL.... I SWAPPED THE AMMO FOR VIBRATORS WHEN WE LOOTED THAT FILTHY CAPITALIST SEX SHOP!"

"IT'S A SAMOAN WARCLUB, MADAM, NOT A HANDY LITTLE DILDO – AND WE DON'T SELL LUBRICATING JELLY!"

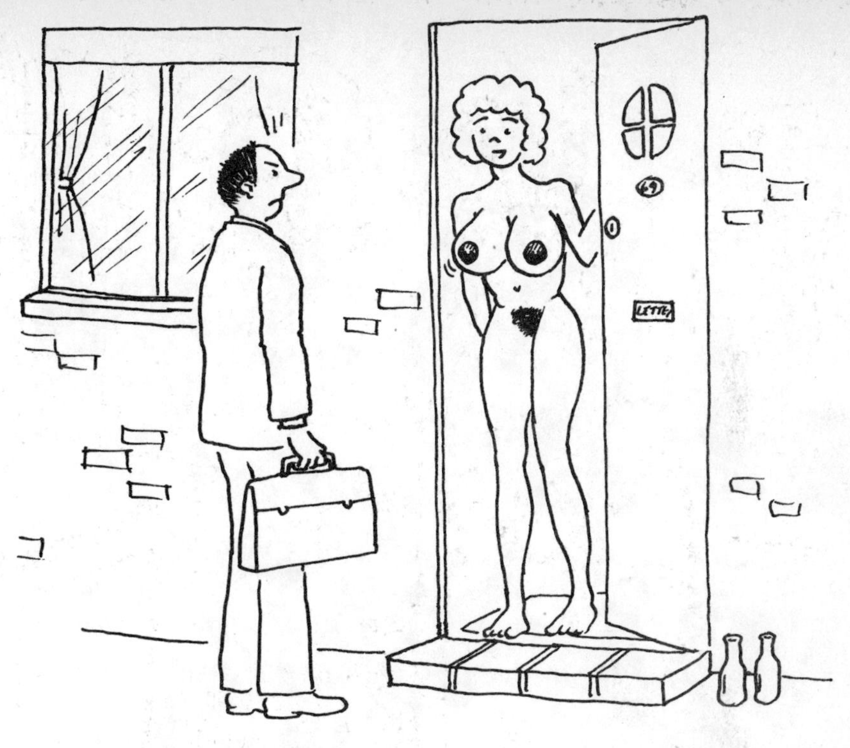

"OH, HELLO DEAR, YOU'RE HOME EARLY — I THOUGHT IT WAS THE INSURANCE MAN."

"YOU'RE SO BLOODY SELFISH, PHYLLIS! I DON'T EVEN LIKE RASPBERRY YOGHURT!"

"NO, MATE I NEVER PRICKED THE SAUSAGES.... BUT I DID SOMETHING DISGUSTING WITH THE BREAD ROLES!"

"I ONCE TOOK A THORN OUT OF HER FOOT, DEAR."

"THE EXPOSURE'S FINE, MISS. NOW WOULD YOU MIND HANDLING MY ENLARGEMENT?"

REMEMBER THE DAYS WHEN THEY JUST USED TO ASK IF YOU WANTED A GOOD TIME, VIC ?
YEH ! NOW IT'S....
UNITED RULE OK!

... FANCY CO-STARRING IN A HOME-MADE BLUE VIDEO ?!?!

"THE HONEYMOON'S BEEN OVER FOR 24 HOURS, DARLING – AND I'VE HAD A HARD DAY AT THE OFFICE . . . ."

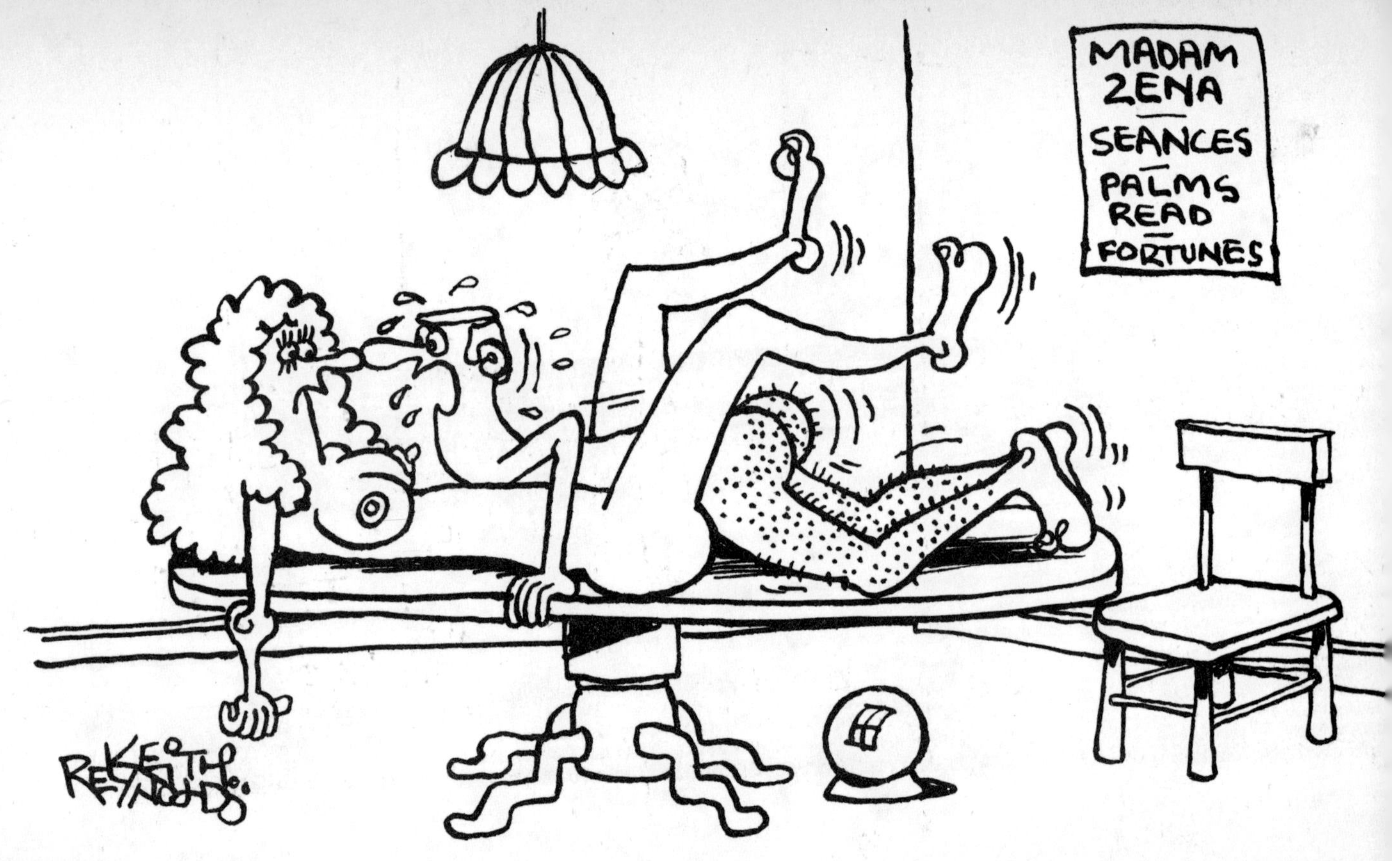

" I WISH YOU'D STOP CALLING OUT 'IS ANYBODY THERE'!"

"NOW YOU JUST FIND SOMEONE TO TYPE IT OUT FOR YOU."

"I KNOW THE WAY TO A MAN'S HEART IS SUPPOSED TO BE THROUGH HIS STOMACH DARLING BUT COULDN'T YOU TRY AIMING A BIT LOWER FROM TIME TO TIME?"

"YOU'RE A BLEEDIN' LIAR, ALFIE GRABBIT – YOU NEVER BOUGHT THIS STUFF AT THE CO-OP!"

"JUST MAKING SURE THAT NOBODY'S STOLEN YOUR MINK COAT, DEAR."

"YOU'RE SURE YOU DON'T MIND MOTHER STAYING OVERNIGHT, DARLING?"

"IT BEATS ME WHAT THEY CAN SEE IN THESE PAGE THREE GIRLS."

"OF COURSE I'LL LOVE YOU ALWAYS, DARLING. WHICH WAY WOULD YOU LIKE TO TRY FIRST?"

" OKAY , MISS DINGLEY , YOU'RE HIRED . NOW, HOW WOULD YOU LIKE TO TRY FOR A RAISE?"

"WHADDYA MEAN .... 'DON'T CALL US, WE'LL CALL YOU'? DO I GET THE PART OF THE NUN OR DON'T I?"

"I KNOW I PROMISED NOT TO BE SO PROMISCUOUS, DEAR – AND AS YOU CAN SEE, I'M TRYING TO CUT DOWN."

"EXCUSE ME, BUT DO YOU DO PRIVATE WORK?"

"I WILL NAE BE LONG, JEANNIE . I'M JUST RINSING OOT THE FRENCH LETTER."

" IT'S AT TIMES LIKE THIS THAT I FEEL LIKE TAKING THE LAW INTO MY OWN HANDS "

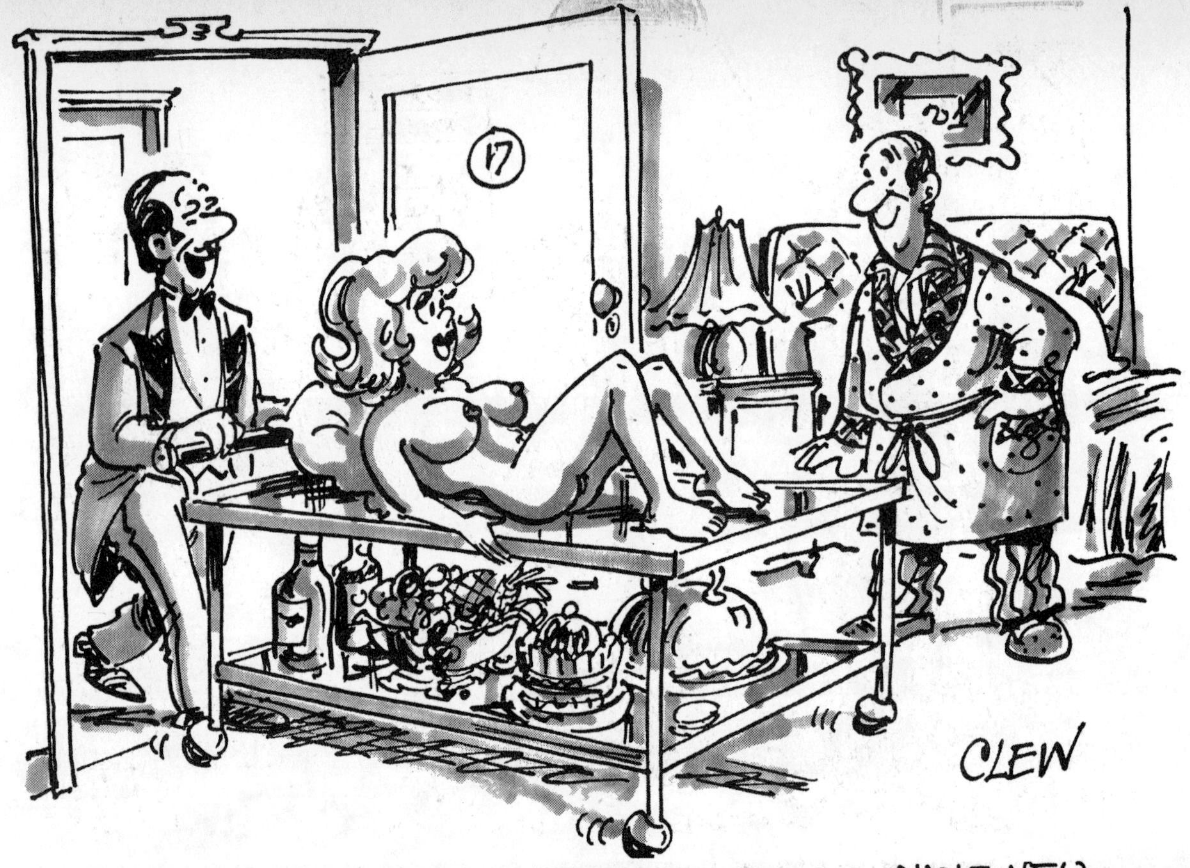

"THE HOTEL MANAGEMENT IS TRYING TO BRING A WHOLE NEW MEANING TO THE WORDS 'ROOM SERVICE'."

"NO WONDER WE'VE HAD SO MANY COMPLAINTS ABOUT YOU, STANLEY. ALL THOSE LADIES MUST HAVE BEEN AWFULLY DISAPPOINTED."

"CONSTABLE DIXON IS HERE TO INVESTIGATE THE OBSCENE PHONE CALLS I'VE BEEN GETTING, DEAR"

"THIS SORT OF BIRD-WATCHING GIVES ME A TALL STALK. YOU COULD SAY I'M A HORNY-THOLOGIST!"

NATURIST CLUB
NO OGLING

BRITISH BIRDS

"SO THE UPSIDE-DOWN SUDSY PACKET ISN'T A SECRET SIGNAL FOR A SWOP 'N' BONDAGE PARTY?"

"MUM - CAN I BORROW THE VIBRATOR TONIGHT ?"

"BUT I *AM*, GIRLS! UNDERNEATH THESE CLOTHES I'M COMPLETELY NAKED!"

"SORRY, SIR - FROM A DISTANCE I COULDN'T TELL YOU WERE USING AN INFLATABLE DUMMY AS A BEACHMAT."

"YOU DON'T HAVE TO HOLD MY BUCKET FOR ME, DAD. IT ISN'T HEAVY."

" THAT'LL TEACH YOU ABOUT BEING UNFAITHFUL TO ME WHEN I'M AWAY FROM HOME ! "

"DO ARCHBISHOPS ALWAYS SAY 'SLIP HER A BIG UN FROM ME, MUSH!' AT ROYAL WEDDINGS?"

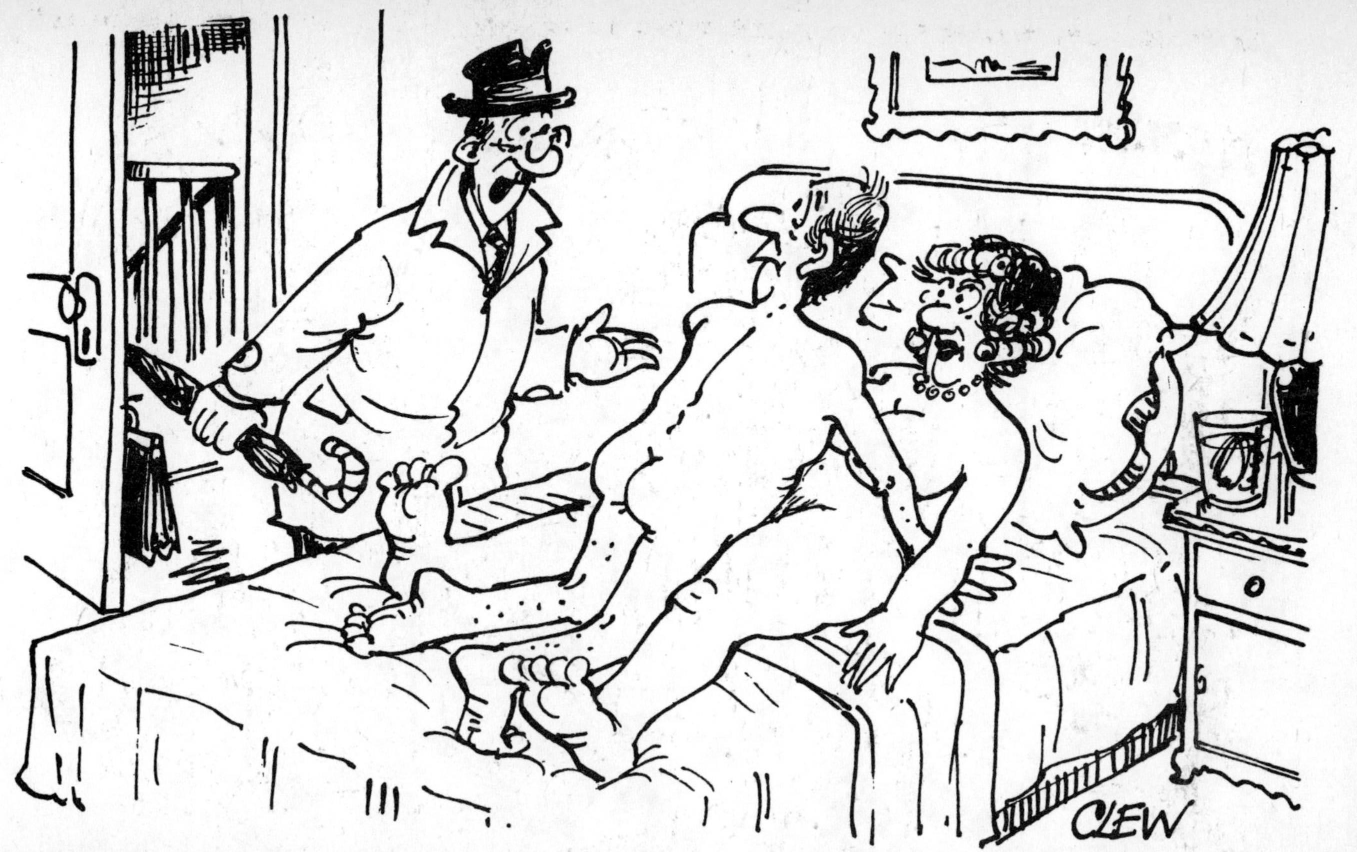

"GOOD GRIEF, HARRY - MY OLD PAL - I <u>HAVE</u> TO! BUT <u>YOU</u> ....?"

"HELLO, DEAR. MISS PLUMM DROPPED HER PEN AND IT'S ROLLED UNDER MY DESK."

" I MUST TRY TO IMPROVE MY SPELLING – HE HAD ME ON THE CARPET AGAIN. "

"WHAT IS IT ABOUT GRANDFATHER'S SILVER CRUET SET THAT ALWAYS MAKES YOU SNIGGER, ELIZA?"